BRITISH
INDEPENDENT BUSES
IN THE 2000s

RICHARD STUBBINGS

AMBERLEY

First published 2020

Amberley Publishing
The Hill, Stroud
Gloucestershire, GL5 4EP

www.amberley-books.com

Copyright © Richard Stubbings, 2020

The right of Richard Stubbings to be identified
as the Author of this work has been asserted in
accordance with the Copyrights, Designs and
Patents Act 1988.

ISBN 978 1 4456 8619 6 (print)
ISBN 978 1 4456 8620 2 (ebook)

British Library Cataloguing in Publication Data.
A catalogue record for this book is available from
the British Library.

Origination by Amberley Publishing.
Printed in the UK.

Introduction

In this book we come roaring through the millennium and into the twenty-first century. With all the changes that had taken place on the bus scene in the last two decades of the twentieth century, many bus enthusiasts, me included, must have been wondering what lay ahead, particularly for the smaller independent operator.

Looking through my photographs, choosing which ones to include in this book, I have been struck by the number of traditional independent operators that I have photographed over the years that are either no longer in operation or have been taken over by, in the most part, the big groups. There are a multitude of reasons for the demise of these firms. In some cases, it was due to retirement with no-one wishing to continue the business. Also, during the early 2000s oil prices rose sharply, as did the labour and insurance costs. This, coupled with falling revenue due to increased traffic congestion and rising car ownership, plus lower council subsidies, meant that a quite a number of smaller independent operators disappeared from our roads. Some were taken over by larger companies and the emerging bigger groups. An example here is the well-known Hedingham and District, now in the hands of the Go-Ahead Group, although they have happily retained the Hedingham name. Other well-known names taken over by larger groups include Truronian in Cornwall, passing to First Group, although again retaining the name, but only on some coaches. Other old-established firms that disappeared during the period of this particular book include Tillingbourne in Surrey, always a favourite of mine, which finished abruptly in 2001 after heavy losses, and Chiltern Queens of Woodcote. Newer operators that disappeared in the 2000s include CMT on Merseyside, passing to Glenvale in 2003 and subsequently to Arriva, and Western Greyhound in Cornwall, which ceased operating in 2015. Metrobus had passed into the hands of the Go-Ahead Group at the end of the 1990s. A very familiar name to disappear, after merging with Shearings, was Wallace Arnold. Indeed, of the ninety-five operators illustrated in this book, fifty-four are, at the time of writing, either no longer in existence or have been swallowed up by larger companies and groups. Happily, there are old-established firms that are still very much with us, not just through the period covered in this book, but at the time of writing, such as Safeguard of Guildford, Yeoman in Hereford and Roselyn in Cornwall.

The vehicles in use with independent operators were changing during the 2000s. Low-floor vehicles, such as the Dennis Dart SLF and the Optare Solo, came into production during the late 1990s, and had begun to appear in the fleets of the independent firms. From 2001 onwards all new public service vehicles with more than twenty-two seats had to be low floor and easily accessible for those using wheelchairs and with restricted mobility, although existing vehicles with step entrances remained in service. This also meant that step-entrance vehicles, such as first-generation Dennis Darts, were passing to smaller operators. When low-floor vehicles became a requirement for operating London Buses contracts, more of this type appeared in larger numbers on high-profile routes run by the bigger firms. Other changes were happening – changes that are not really obvious from photographs – such as the move to cleaner engines built to Euro standards that were constantly being updated. The larger companies, particularly in urban areas, were beginning to trial hybrid vehicles, using both an electric engine and a diesel engine – certainly a sign of things to come.

I have found it interesting, when choosing the photographs for this and my previous books, observing how vehicles have changed over the years. At the beginning of the period covered by my first book – the 1980s – vehicles such as the Western Greyhound Bristol VR, illustrated in the pages of this volume, were newly into service with their original operators. Now, with the swift rate of change to vehicle design, buses and coaches, illustrated in this book covering the 2000s, are in turn entering preservation. Back in the 1980s it was very common for a small operator, particularly a rural one, to regularly turn out a coach on a bus service, whereas in the 2000s, with step entrances on service buses gradually being phased out, it was more likely to be a modern purpose-built service bus with low floor easy access, something that is, of course, now mandatory.

For this book, covering the 2000s, I have selected photographs up to the end of 2010. I was still very much based in the south-east in this period, with occasional forays into other areas. As previously, I have tried to give the sense of going on a journey around the country, starting and finishing in Guildford where I was based for so long, moving westwards to my beloved West Country, then up the west side of the England and back down the east, covering East Anglia, the Home Counties, London and the south-east.

Again, I must acknowledge the information provided by *Bus View* and Wikipedia for vehicle and operator information, as well as my collection of *Buses* magazines, *Buses Yearbooks* and *Buses Annuals*. The few other publications I have referred to are acknowledged elsewhere.

I must also thank my mother Sylvia and my brother Michael for their encouragement of both my hobby and the writing of these books. I must also thank my sons David and Peter for putting up with their father disappearing off to photograph buses all the time, especially when it was supposed to be a train-spotting trip! I must especially thank my partner Debs for helping and encouraging me in the writing of these books, proofreading the text for me, suggesting alterations and for just being there.

These first few photographs of the vehicles in the fleet of Safeguard, Guildford, in many ways trace the move from traditional step-entrance vehicles to low-floor easy-access buses during the 2000s. In this view we see Leyland Tiger C164SPB, leaving Guildford's Friary bus station for Park Barn, on 2 September 2000. It carries the last Duple Dominant bus body bought by Safeguard and is now preserved. The Duple Dominant bus body became the Safeguard standard, mainly on Leyland Leopard and Leyland Tiger chassis, although their first was on a Bedford YRQ in 1974; there was a second-hand AEC as well.

An interesting Dennis Dart to enter Safeguard's fleet in January 2000 was H577 MOC. Starting life as London United DT77, it passed for a short time to Warner of Tewkesbury. Upon sale to Safeguard its Carlyle body was modified with a Plaxton Pointer front. In this form it served Guildford for about ten years. Seen here in the Friary bus station on 26 October 2000, bound for Boxgrove Park, it is another Safeguard vehicle that has now been preserved.

In 2000 Safeguard started operating the free town centre shuttle on behalf of Guildford Borough Council. This led to the purchase of their first low-floor vehicles, namely two Dennis Dart SLFs with twenty-nine-seat Plaxton Pointer 2 bodies, these being the largest vehicles that were able to negotiate some of the smaller roads in the town. Here we see V946 DNB, wearing the town shuttle livery, leaving the Friary bus station on 26 October 2000.

Subsequent low-floor vehicles, with one exception, were Optares. After purchasing two Optare Excels from Tillingbourne when that company sadly collapsed, they bought YJ03 UMM, pictured here at the Southsea Spectacular, on 8 June 2003. All three Excels continue in service with Safeguard at the time of writing.

A relatively rare vehicle that joined Safeguard's coach fleet in 1996 was WPF 926, a Neoplan with a Plaxton Paramount 4000 body. Starting life in 1986 on National Express work with South Wales Transport, it was registered SWN 159. After being sold by them in 1989, it moved through a succession of operators before arriving in Surrey. Pictured here parked near Guildford station on 18 February 2001, it was withdrawn at the end of the year.

Countryliner, the coaching arm of London and Country, which in turn came under Arriva, was purchased in a management buyout in 1998. During 2001 the company moved into bus operation, as seen here with Plaxton Beaver-bodied Mercedes-Benz Vario V991 DNB, leaving Guildford's Friary bus station on service 463 on 31 July 2001.

In the early 2000s Countryliner started to update their coach fleet with some new Mercedes-Benz coaches. Here BU03 LXV, a Mercedes-Benz Touro, is seen taking part in the Brighton Coach Rally on 12 April 2003. I got to know Countryliner quite well as their coaches were often hired to transport the county youth orchestra, where I was a tutor, to concerts.

One company that only just survived into the 2000s before closing suddenly was Tillingbourne Bus. Always a favourite firm of mine, they expanded their operations considerably and invested heavily in an up-to-date fleet. Seen here on 25 October 2000, loading in The Forbury, Reading, for its journey to Arborfield on service 144 – both places well out of their original operating area – is L103 EPA, a Northern Counties Paladin-bodied Dennis Dart.

Optare Vectas became popular with Tillingbourne, who ended up with five in their fleet. Here, photographed in Guildford's Friary bus station on 13 January 2001, is P107 OPX, laying over after arriving on service 21.

Tillingbourne also bought second-hand vehicles. A particularly interesting one was E364 NEG, a Volvo B10M-61 that started life with Premier Travel carrying a Plaxton Paramount body. It was rebodied in 1992 with this Northern Counties Paladin body and served for about six years with Tillingbourne. It is seen here on 2 September 2000 in North Street, Guildford, arriving on service 24 from Cranleigh.

Seen on 2 February 2000 at Kingsmead, Farnborough, working on local service 48, is R505 WRV, one of a number of Optare Metroriders in the Tillingbourne fleet. Over the 1990s Tillingbourne built a sizable network of services in north-east Hampshire.

One of two Optare Excels bought by Tillingbourne, X308 CBT is seen in Guildford Friary bus station on 13 January 2001, working service 25 to Cranleigh, about three months before closure. This vehicle, along with its sister X307 CBT, passed to Safeguard of Guildford, with whom it is still in service.

An operator that started up in Surrey and lasted a mere five years was Surrey Rider. Seen in Sutton Green on 26 March 2000 heading for Camberley is Dennis Lance K322 YJA, fitted with a Northern Counties Paladin body, and formerly LN22 in the fleet of Metroline.

Seen on 26 October 2000, this time in Guildford Friary bus station, was former Bristol Omnibus Leyland National 2 AAE 647V, working on service 478 to Sheerwater.

Former Volvo demonstrator N101 HGO, a B6BLE with Wright Crusader, stayed barely a month in the Surrey Rider fleet before moving on. It is seen here in the Friary bus station, Guildford, on 11 February 2001.

Northdown was the name used by Nostalgiabus for their everyday bus services, as distinct from the services using their heritage fleet. Optare Solo Y867 PWT was new in July 2001 and is seen here on 2 September 2001 in Guildford, bound for Kingston.

Another operator that only lasted a very few years in the Guildford area, but who managed in their short life to build up a considerable fleet, was White Rose, based in Staines. Seen in North Street on 2 September 2001 was V675 FPO, a Dennis Dart SLF with UVG Urbanstar body.

White Rose acquired H103 MOB in June 2000. A Carlyle-bodied Dennis Dart, it is seen in Onslow Street, Guildford, on 26 October 2000 on service 1 to Onslow Village.

South of Guildford and into West Sussex we find Compass Bus, based in the seaside town of Worthing. Founded in the early 1990s, it has now grown to become one of the major independent operators in the south-east. Seen in Horsham Carfax, on 9 May 2010, is Optare Solo MX54 KXR on a Sunday working of local route 98. A blast from the past can be seen behind in the form of a preserved Southdown Leyland Titan PD3.

Laying over at Worthing Pier on 23 May 2010 we find Transbus Dart SLF GX54 AWH. Darts like this were the mainstay of the fleet for a long time until the appearance of the Enviro.

An operator a little further along the coast, on the Hampshire/West Sussex border, was Emsworth & District. Seen on Hayling Island on 30 May 2001 was former City of Oxford Optare Metrorider G778 WFC, working the Hayling Hoppa.

Taking part in the Southsea Spectacular on 8 June 2003 was Leyland Titan A883 SUL. Delivered new to London Transport as their T883, it was bought by Emsworth & District in May 2001 and converted to single door.

Moving north through Hampshire we return to Farnborough, where we see Frimley Coaches P403 KAV, a fairly rare Marshall Minibus new to London General as their ML13, at Kingsmead on service 80 to Fleet, 24 August 2001.

Brijan Tours of Curdridge, near Eastleigh, operated a mixture of local bus services and private hires. Seen at their depot in Curdridge on 18 April 2010 is former East Kent MCW Metrobus UVY 412. Originally registered F764 EKM, it joined Brijan in 2000.

Also seen on 18 April 2010 at the depot were two former London Transport vehicles, Leyland Titan TIL 4557, previously registered A942 SYE as T942, and Leyland Olympian EIG 9487, formerly C121 CHM and numbered L121.

Moving down into Southampton we find Princess of West End operating F370 BUA, an Optare Delta, formerly a demonstrator, on the Uni-link service on 27 January 2001. I had photographed this vehicle previously, when it was in the fleet of Seamarks of Luton.

Marchwood Motorways, whose origins can be traced back to the 1940s, had a franchising agreement with Solent Blue Line to operate vehicles in their livery on two Southampton city routes. Numbered 505 in the Solent Blue Line fleet is Marchwood's L510 EHD, an Ikarus-bodied DAF SB220, seen here in Bargate Street, Southampton, in 2002.

Marchwood took delivery of a number of low-floor DAF SB120s, with Wright Cadet bodies, in 2003 for use on the franchised services in Southampton. Seen at a rally in Winchester on 27 April 2003 and numbered 551 in the Solent Blue Line fleet is Marchwood's YG52 CME.

An example of Marchwood's coach fleet is R64 GNW, a DAF SB3000 with Van Hool Alizee body, seen here at The Hard in Portsmouth on 10 August 2000.

A visitor from the Isle of Wight, seen on 10 August 2000 at The Hard in Portsmouth, with the masts of HMS Victory in the background, was T810 RDL of Solent Travel in Newport, a MAN 18.310 with Noge bodywork.

Bluebird Coaches of Weymouth can trace its origins back to the 1920s. It has always been primarily an operator of tours and private hires. Our trips to visit family in the West Country from the south-east often entailed a stop at Shaftesbury, and it was here that on 21 April 2003 I photographed A15 FRX, a Volvo B10M with Plaxton Premiere 320 body, delivered new to Frames Rickards of London and originally registered M429 WAK. It moved to the Dorset coast in 2001.

A well-known and well-respected name in the coaching world was Excelsior of Bournemouth. Their Volvo B10M A4 EXC, carrying a Plaxton Excalibur body, is seen here at Heathrow Airport on 2 September 2002.

Excelsior became part of the Flights Group in the late 1990s, and their livery changed to the one carried here by A17 XEL, based upon Flights own livery. A Volvo B10M with Plaxton Premiere 350 body, it is seen at Bournemouth station on 31 August 2000 on a National Express working.

As previously mentioned, Excelsior also operated on the National Express network. Seen here wearing the Flightlink livery and entering Poole bus station on 1 September 2001 is A7 XCL, a Volvo B10M with Plaxton Paragon body.

A much-missed name in my native Somerset is Safeway of South Petherton. Leyland Leopard GIB 5970 originally carried a Willowbrook Spacecar body, and was new to National Travel North West as XCW 153R. After serving with a number of operators in Lancashire, it passed to Safeway and was rebodied with this rather boxy Willowbrook Warrior bus body. It is seen leaving Yeovil bus station for Crewkerne on 8 August 2001.

Parked in Newquay on 18 August 2002, was Safeway's Duple 320-bodied Leyland Tiger coach E565 YYA. Sadly, Safeway ceased trading in 2007.

Moving on down into Devon and to the cathedral city of Exeter, we find Dartline Coaches providing local services as well as coach hire. Seen in Belgrave Road on 2 January 2002, with the former Devon General garage behind, is Marshall-bodied Iveco Daily S926 KOD. This company has expanded and continues to operate at the time of writing.

Dawlish Coaches came into being in the early 1960s. Whilst being primarily a coach operator, they did also operate a small number of buses over the years. Seen here on 14 August 2001 is X424 CFJ, a Mercedes-Benz Vario with Plaxton Beaver body operating on a local service in its hometown.

Dawlish operated a top-of-the-range coach fleet, often on touring work for travel agencies. Seen here in Truro on New Year's Day 2003, wearing Majestic Tours livery, is Bova Futura W157 RYB. Dawlish Coaches ceased trading in 2010.

It was not uncommon to see vehicles of independent companies operating on hire to National Express during the busy summer months. Seen here on 11 August 2001, parked on Marcus Hill, Newquay, while duplicating a service to Bristol, is Hookways of Meeth 789 FAY. Delivered new to Jennings of Bude as D36 LRL, this Duple 340-bodied Volvo B10M passed to Hookways when they took over Jennings in 1998. This firm ceased operation in 2011.

The lovely village of Dalwood, on the edge of the Blackdown Hills, is the home of Sewards Coaches. Seen in Exeter bus station on 17 August 2001 is their R609 OTA, a MAN 11.220 with a short Berkhof Axial body, working on Sewards service 302 to Exeter.

Turner of Chulmleigh operated a service from that village on Dartmoor into Exeter. Working the route on 17 August 2001 was J398 GKH, a Dennis Dart with Plaxton Pointer body, formerly with Metroline as their DR98. Over the years Turners have built up their network of bus services linking villages with places like Exeter.

Kingdom's of Tiverton have been in operation since the early 1960s, operating a mixture of mainly private hires and tours and school services. Using the 'Tivvy Coaches' fleetname is TIL 9833, a Volvo B10M-60 with Van Hool Alizee body. Bought from Shearings and formerly registered J218 NNC, it is seen in Bideford on 13 August 2001.

A company that could trace its ancestry back to the 1940s was Heard of Hartland. Seen here on a private hire to Penzance on 29 April 2000 is P887 FMO, a Dennis Javelin with Berkhof Axial body, bought from Limebourne of London in 1998.

A major operator from Plymouth, seen here on a private hire to Dawlish on 14 August 2001, is Target Travel H371 VCG, a Volvo B10M with Plaxton Paramount 3500 III body. It started life as H818 AHS in the well-known Scottish fleet of Parks of Hamilton.

Taw and Torridge Coaches of Merton, near Okehampton, came into being in the mid-1970s. Seen here on 5 January 2001 by Victoria coach station is 775 HOD, a Van Hool Alicron, delivered new to Pettigrew of Kirkoswald in Cumbria as G254 VML, and bought by Taw and Torridge in 1993. It is duplicating National Express service 502.

Trathens Travel Services came under the control of Parks of Hamilton in 1996. They had been co-operating with National Express since the mid-1980s; however, their vehicles were now wearing National Express livery rather than Trathens' own colours. In this view Van Hool Astromega R261 OFJ is seen leaving Victoria coach station on 5 January 2001 at the start of its long run to Penzance on National Express service 504.

Trathens was a keen operator of double-deck coaches. Here Neoplan Skyliner YN51 XMU is seen on Buckingham Palace Road on 17 April 2003, heading for Fleetwood on National Express service 570. The Trathens name was dropped in 2009.

The family owned Roselyn Coaches, of Par in Cornwall, has a long and proud history stretching back to 1947. It rapidly became a favourite company of mine and a visit to their depot on trips to see my parents was a must! Photographed at the depot in Par on 29 August 2000, this former East Midland Bristol VRT, BCV 9IT, is, as far as I know, the only VR ever to carry a Cornish registration, having been reregistered from AET 186T in 1998.

The Bristol VRs were gradually replaced by Leyland Olympians and here we see JNZ 2425 at the depot in Par, on 5 April 2010. An all-Leyland Olympian, it was delivered new to London United as G311 UYK, and numbered L311 before passing to East Yorkshire, in whose livery it is seen here, as its 653. The Plaxton-bodied Volvo parked next to it, YAF 872, bears the registration first seen in my 1980s book on a Bedford YRQ belonging to Ford of Gunnislake. It was carried by a total of three vehicles in that fleet before being transferred to this former Wallace Arnold coach, new as T519 EUB.

Seen on a private hire to Penzance on 23 August 2000 is Roselyn's 728 FDV. A Volvo B10M with Plaxton Paramount 3500 II body, it started life as B706 WUA in the fleet of Dodsworth of Boroughbridge, before passing to Moffat and Williamson of Gauldry in Fife. It made the move to Cornwall in 1998.

Lasting barely a year in the Roselyn fleet, D126 HML, a Bedford YNV Venturer with Duple Laser 2 body, arrived in Par in 2003. It is seen here at the depot on 12 April 2004.

This Volvo B12M was the fifth vehicle in the Roselyn fleet to bear the registration 244 AJB, originally carried on a former AERE AEC Regent V. Fitted with a Van Hool Alizee T9 body and originally registered WA04 MHJ, this coach was purchased by Roselyn from Chalfont Coaches in 2008 and is seen at the depot in Par on 5 April 2010.

The family-run business of Hopley, based at Mount Hawke, took delivery of P87 SAF for their Porthtowan to Truro service in 1997. A Volvo B10B with Wright Endurance body, it is seen in Truro bus station on 29 December 2001. This vehicle passed to Delaine of Bourne in 2003.

Bristol VR KVF 248V was new to Eastern Counties as VR248 before passing to Cambus and then to Viscount. It then found its way to South Wales, serving with Red and White before purchase by Hopleys. It is seen in Truro bus station on 9 August 2001 on the Porthtowan service, in Hopleys livery applied in Stagecoach style.

Seen at the Porthtowan Beach terminus of service 304 to Truro is Hopley's IAZ 2314, 18 February 2004. Delivered new to National Welsh as HR1858, and registered MUH 288X, this ECW-bodied Leyland Olympian spent some time with Luton and District before migrating to Cornwall in 2002.

Seen here leaving Truro bus station for Porthtowan on 27 August 2003, WK0 3BTE is one of three Optare Solos delivered to Hopleys that year as their first low-floor vehicles.

Truronian's double-decker of choice during the 1990s and early 2000s was the Bristol VR. Seen here on Lemon Quay, Truro, on 18 August 2002, in school bus livery but working a park and ride service is SNN 158R, a former East Midland vehicle.

Bound for The Lizard on 21 August 2000, and under looming stormy clouds, is Truronian's P454 SCV, one of four Dennis Dart SLFs with Plaxton Pointer bodies delivered in 1997.

Truronian took delivery of two Dennis Dart SLFs in 2001. Fitted with Plaxton Pointer 2 bodies, they carried a dedicated livery and appropriate registrations; in this case Y2 EDN, for a service from Newquay bus station, where it is seen on 11 August 2001, to the Eden Project.

Truronian also undertook work on behalf of National Express, as seen here by L338 WAF, arriving in Plymouth on 22 August 2000. A Caetano Algarve-bodied Volvo B10M, it is bound for Brighton on service 315.

National Express work took Truronian's vehicles far and wide. Seen here on Marcus Hill, Newquay, on 11 August 2001, is M372 CRL, a Volvo B10M with Plaxton Premiere 350 body heading for Manchester on service 329.

Truronian did operate a few vehicles in National Express livery, such as N498 PYS. A former Parks of Hamilton Volvo B10M with Van Hool Alizee body, it is seen here leaving Plymouth's Bretonside bus station for Brighton, on 17 August 2002.

Parked in Truro on 2 April 2002 on more mundane work is W3 TRU, a Volvo B10M with Plaxton Panther body. Truronian was taken over by First Group in 2008. Happily, though, the name is still carried on members of the coach fleet.

Palmer of Blackwater operated under the Wheal Briton name. Their Plaxton Paramount-bodied Scania K7 DTS is seen here on Cliff Road, Newquay, on 28 August 2000.

St Brannock's Travel of Newquay were connected with a hotel of the same name in Newquay. Their fleet consisted of two Volvo B10Ms with Jonckheere Deauville 45 bodies that originated with Bebb of Llantwit Fardre. One of them, L91 GAX, is seen here in Truro on 18 August 2000. This vehicle and sister coach L93 GAX joined the fleet in December 1996 and stayed until operations ceased in 2006.

Oates Travel is a small family-run business based in St Ives that specialises in day tours around the wonderful duchy of Cornwall, an area I got to know and love during the twenty years my parents lived there. Seen here in Newquay on 28 August 2003 is M662 BAF, a Volvo B10M with Van Hool Alizee body.

Western Greyhound was founded in 1997 and grew rapidly to prominence as services provided by other operators dwindled. Seen sporting their original pink and white livery is former Southdown Bristol VRT JWV 259W, photographed on Cliff Road, Newquay, on 11 August 2001.

Caught again on Cliff Road, Newquay, this time on 28 August 2000, is a member of Western Greyhound's small coach fleet, 674 SHY. Originally registered RDF 500R, this Leyland Leopard with Plaxton Supreme Express body was new to Pulham's of Bourton-on-the-Water in 1976.

The Mercedes-Benz Vario with Plaxton Beaver very swiftly became the workhorse of the Western Greyhound fleet as it was ideal for negotiating the narrow Cornish lanes. Also photographed on Cliff Road, Newquay, on 11 August 2001, S503 SRL is bound for St Eval.

Western Greyhound's livery changed to green and white in the early 2000s. Seen in Boscawen Street, Truro, on 27 August 2003, is X33 WGL, another Mercedes-Benz Vario, bound for Wadebridge.

Seen in Newquay bus station on 18 August 2010 is BU53 ZWZ, a Mercedes-Benz Citaro that came to Western Greyhound from Worth of Enstone in Oxfordshire. Sadly, a major fire at the company's main depot in Summercourt in 2013 destroyed a large proportion of the fleet, including this vehicle.

Western Greyhound's fleet of Bristol VRTs were gradually replaced in the early 2000s by Volvo Olympians, many of which, like S454 ATV, came from Nottingham City Transport. Carrying an East Lancs body, it is seen in Newquay bus station on 18 August 2010.

Low-floor double-deckers arrived in the Western Greyhound fleet in the shape of Plaxton President-bodied Dennis Tridents such as WK51 CAL, seen here leaving Newquay for Truro on 18 August 2010. New to Go-Ahead Northern as NK51 UCV it reached Western Greyhound by way of City of Oxford, who registered it R6 OXF. By the end of 2009 Western Greyhound were the biggest operator in Cornwall.

A major operator in the South West is Berrys of Taunton. One of their Van Hool Alizee-bodied Volvo B10Ms, PIB 4019, is seen here on 28 August 2000 travelling along Cliff Road, Newquay. Delivered new as D547 OYD in 1987, it stayed in the fleet until 2016.

A Somerset operator no longer with us is Bryant's of Williton. Their Bedford YNT B655 BYB, carrying a Plaxton Paramount 3200 body, is seen at Minehead station on a service to Blue Anchor on 23 March 2002. The driver is issuing a ticket from what looks like an old Setright ticket machine.

Parked in Newquay on New Year's Day in 2001 was Bakers of Weston-super-Mare WJI 6879. This Van Hool Alizee-bodied Volvo B10M was new to Travellers of Hounslow as F552 TMH, before passing to Silcox of Pembroke Dock. It joined the Bakers fleet in February 1998 and stayed there until 2009.

Turners of Bristol were established in the mid-1960s as a family-run coach business. Their silver-coloured coaches are a familiar sight in the Bristol area and further afield, as evident here with S60CJT, seen turning into Buckingham Palace Road. This Volvo B10M with Berkhof Axial body was on National Express work when photographed on 5 January 2001.

Willetts of Pillowell in the Forest of Dean is a family-run business that can trace its roots back ninety years. On 14 August 2001, during what was primarily a train-spotting trip to Dawlish, I caught this Setra from the Willetts' fleet, 890 CVJ, on a private hire. Originally registered N200 TCC, this vehicle arrived with the company in 1998 from the fleet of Brelaton of Hounslow, who traded as the Travellers Coach Company.

Trips to Wales were few and far between for me during the period of this book. However, I still came across Welsh vehicles, such as X46 CNY, belonging to the Bebb of Llantwit Fardre fleet, adorned in National Express livery. A Volvo B10M with Plaxton Paragon body, it is seen on 5 March 2001 leaving Victoria coach station for Cardiff on service 509.

Other vehicles from Bebb's fleet were also pressed into service on National Express duties. Caught as it exited Victoria coach station on 1 September 2003 is CA52 LBG, a Volvo B12M with a Sunsundegui Sideral body. Bebb passed to the Veolia Group in late 2005.

D Coaches of Morriston operated tours from their South Wales base under the Diamond name. Seen outside Taunton bus station on 2 January 2001 is their P724 JYA, an Iveco Eurorider with Beulas Stergo body.

Shamrock of Pontypridd became a major provider of bus services in South Wales as well as operating tours and private hires. In this shot, taken on 10 August 2001 in Bretonside, Plymouth, outside the bus station, we see Berkhof Axial-bodied Volvo B10M R921 ULA. Shamrock ceased operations in 2006, passing, like Bebb, to the Veolia Group.

Jones of Pwllheli in Caernarfonshire operate under the Caelloi Motors name and can trace their origins back to the 1850s. An operator of tours, day excursions and private hires from their North Wales base I photographed this smart Plaxton Premiere 350-bodied Volvo B10M, N418 EJC, at The Hard in Portsmouth on 10 August 2000.

Family in Herefordshire meant visits to that lovely county, and more photographic opportunities. Seen in front of Ledbury's seventeenth-century Market House on 29 August 2001 is Leyland National MOI 5055 from the fleet of DRM of Bromyard. Originally London Buses LS323 (AYR 323T), and now minus its distinctive roof pod, it is at the Ledbury terminus of service 476 from Hereford.

Seen at the Hereford end of service 476, in the country bus station, is DRM's MOI 4000, caught the day before the Leyland National. New to Parks of Hamilton as G68 RGG, this vehicle's original Plaxton Paramount body was burnt out whilst in service with Knowles of Paignton. It was subsequently purchased by DRM in 1994 who rebodied it with this East Lancs bus body.

The major operator in Hereford is Yeomans. Seen in Hereford Country bus station on 29 August 2001 is J74 CVJ, an Alexander Dash-bodied Dennis Dart, laying over before heading for Kington on service 439.

Also parked in Hereford's Country bus station that day was P71 MOV, waiting to depart for Almeley on service 446. A Dennis Lance with Northern Counties Paladin body, it arrived with Yeomans in 1999 from Serverse of Mile Oak.

Yeomans had a wide variety of vehicles in Hereford on 29 August 2001. This former Bristol Omnibus Bristol VRT, EWS 743W, was bound for Madley on service 449.

Seen in Hereford, again on 29 August 2001, is Yeoman's first low-floor vehicle, Optare Excel X533 NWT, new in 2000. It is seen here awaiting its departure time on service 454 to Fownhope.

Yeomans also undertook work on behalf of National Express, as seen here on 17 April 2003 on Buckingham Palace Road. YN03 NJJ is a Volvo B12M with Plaxton Paragon body.

30 August 2001 found Lugg Valley Primrose of Leominster's J249 SOC laying over in Hereford Country bus station. Working service 501 from Leominster, it is a Carlyle-bodied Dennis Dart, new to Cave of Shirley.

Horlick and Harris of Ross-on-Wye operated into Hereford on service 37. On 30 August 2001 the allocated vehicle was D105 TFT, a former Busways Carlyle bodied-Freight Rover Sherpa.

An unusual vehicle, seen here in the fleet of Sargeants of Kington, is H918 SCX, a Talbot Freeway that they bought from the Sheffield Employment Service in 1995. It is seen here on 30 August 2001 in Hereford Country bus station on service 905.

One of Sargeants' first low-floor vehicles was this Optare Excel, W408 UCJ, seen here leaving Hereford Country bus station at the start of its journey back to its home village of Kington on 20 August 2001.

The small fleet of Powell of Ledbury operated under the name of Newbury Coaches and were always very smartly turned out. Pictured at their depot on 29 August 2001 was F803 KCJ, a Dennis Javelin with Plaxton Paramount 3200 III body.

Also parked in the depot that day was former Wallace Arnold Volvo B10M G518 LWU, also with a Plaxton Paramount body, but this time an example of the taller 3500 model.

Parked opposite the depot on 29 August 2001 was N128 DDT, another Volvo B10M this time with a Plaxton Premiere 350 body. This vehicle arrived with Newbury Coaches from Godson of Crossgates in West Yorkshire in April 2001. Newbury Coaches ceased operations in 2016.

Photographed on 29 August 2001 against the backdrop of Ledbury's lovely seventeenth-century Market House is Bromyard Omnibus BWP 788M, working on service 672 from Bromyard to Ledbury. This Leyland Leopard PSU4 originally carried a Duple Dominant coach body and was new to National Welsh as RBO 194M before being sold to Davies, Pencader, who re-registered it UCK 500 – a registration originally carried on a Ribble Leyland Leopard – and rebodied it with this Willowbrook Warrior body in 1989. It passed to the Bromyard Omnibus fleet of Martin Perry in 2001.

Seen in Worcester bus station on 29 August 2001 is Bromyard Omnibus J656 REY, a Mercedes-Benz 811D with a Wright body, bound for Cradley on service 417. Worcester is also home to one of the most scenic cricket grounds in the country as well as the birthplace of Sir Edward Elgar, one of England's greatest composers and a personal favourite.

Astons of Worcester operated W631 RNP, a very colourful Plaxton Pointer 2-bodied Dennis Dart SLF, on service 382 to Pershore. It is seen leaving Worcester bus station on 29 August 2001.

Despite its registration, J2 NNC is actually a 1994 Mercedes-Benz 711D with a Plaxton body. Delivered new to Hardings of Betchworth in Surrey as L2 HCT, it was reregistered L568 WGC upon sale to Cresswell of Evesham in 1999, who then re-registered it again to J2 NNC, the letters being the initials of the founder of the company, N. N. Cresswell. It is seen here on 29 August 2001 leaving Worcester bus station for Sedgeberrow on service 565.

A trip to Warwick for an orchestral engagement on 9 March 2002 gave me an opportunity for a little photography. Seen here in Market Street, and wearing Countylinks livery, is X432 KON, a Mercedes-Benz Citaro from the fleet of Johnson, Henley-in-Arden. It is working on service 555.

Wainfleet of Nuneaton sent their former Parks of Hamilton Volvo B10M MIW 5788 to Devon in 2001, where I photographed it in Dawlish on 14 August. Carrying a Plaxton Paramount 3500 III body, it was originally registered G87 RGG. Sadly, Wainfleet did not survive the decade, ceasing to trade in 2006.

Diamond Bus was the name given to the bus operations of the Birmingham Coach Company. Seen outside New Street station, Birmingham, on 26 July 2002, is former Metrobus Dennis Dart J702 EMX operating service 16 to Hamstead, the company's original route that it started working in 1986 upon de-regulation.

Working the same route on the same day was this Wright-bodied DAF SB120, YJ51 EKB, delivered new to the company in 2001. Diamond Bus became part of the Go-Ahead Group at the end of 2005 and subsequently part of Rotala where the name Diamond Bus is still used.

Pete's Travel was the trading name of Probus Management, which started operating in 1994 using a fleet of minibuses. The Dennis Dart then became the standard vehicle, as shown here by S772 RNE, a Dart SLF with Plaxton Pointer 2 body. It was new to Pete's Travel in 1998. The company was purchased by Go-Ahead in 2006 and merged into the Go West Midlands fleet with Diamond Bus, which was in turn sold to Rotala in 2008. S772 RNE was photographed outside Birmingham's New Street station on 26 July 2002 whilst on a train-spotting trip with my eldest son.

Coaches from the West Midlands-based Bowens Group were to be found all over the country. Caught in Plymouth's Bretonside bus station on 10 August 2001 was Bova Futura K297 GDT, seen whilst working a tour based on Torquay.

Seen in the Tolcarne coach park in Newquay, on 17 February 2004, is Bowens R637 VNN, a MAN 18.310 with Noge Catalan body. Bowens ceased trading in 2012.

Coaches from the Midlands are frequently to be spotted in the West Country. Seen in Truro on 4 April 2002 is T894 HBF, a Volvo B10M with Van Hool Alizee T9 body from the fleet of Bassetts Coaches of Tittensor, near Stoke-on-Trent. The following year Bassetts decided to pull out of the world of coaching and concentrate on road haulage, with this particular vehicle passing to Preston Bus.

A trip to Liverpool for an orchestral audition in 2001 presented me with an opportunity to photograph the busy, varied bus scene in that city. Liverpool Motor Service was the fleetname of Forrest of Aintree, operating a smartly turned out fleet of green and cream vehicles. Photographed in Queen Square, Liverpool, on 22 February was former Ribble Leyland National 2 DBV 834W, working on service 14B to Broadway.

Working on the same route on the same day was B551 ATX, a former Cardiff East Lancs-bodied Leyland Olympian. This vehicle was sold to Stephenson's of Easingwold, North Yorkshire in September 2001.

Merseyline Travel built up a large fleet of secondhand double-deckers – mainly former West Midlands Leyland Fleetlines plus a few Bristol VRs and a number of single-deck Leyland Lynxes. However, their fleet did also include five former Greater Manchester MCW Metrobuses, one of which, ANA 155Y, is seen here in Queen Square, Liverpool, on 22 February 2001.

CMT started life as a coach operator before diversifying into bus operation at the time of deregulation in the 1980s. It initially used a fleet of Leyland Nationals. From the mid-1990s onwards CMT invested in a large number of both new vehicles and quite modern secondhand types to replace the Nationals. One of the secondhand purchases was M393 VWX, a Volvo B10B with Alexander Strider body that arrived from Harrogate and District at the end of 2000. It is seen here in Queen Square, Liverpool, on 22 February 2001.

Seen here crossing Queen Square on 22 February 2001, surrounded by Arriva vehicles on its way to Netherley on service 79, Leyland Lynx 2077, G221 DKA, was new to Halton Transport in Widnes before spending some time with Isle of Man National Transport as MAN94F. It had been with CMT for about a month when this shot was taken.

The investment in the fleet included low-floor vehicles such as 2037, S448 KCW, a Volvo B10BLE with Wright Renown body, seen here in Queen Square, Liverpool, on 22 February 2001 on service 12 to Stockbridge Village. CMT was purchased by Glenvale Transport in 2003, who in turn joined the Stagecoach empire in 2005.

A well-known and highly respected name on the streets of Preston and the surrounding area was that of J. Fishwick and Sons, founded in 1907. Being based in Leyland they standardised on Leylands for many years, but then turned to DAF/VDL vehicles. This is shown here by their number 2, YJ09 CVF, a VDL SB200 with Wright Pulsar body, seen on 4 September 2010 in Fishergate, Preston, heading home to Leyland on service 111.

Seen on the same day, at the same spot, on the same route, was number 39, YG52 EVY, a DAF SB200 with the earlier Wright Commander body. Sadly, Fishwicks ceased trading in 2015.

The blue coaches of Shearings are a familiar sight all over the country. They are based in Wigan but operate from depots situated nationwide. Allocated to the depot in Tunbridge Wells, and seen at Hampton Court station on 14 June 2000, M660 KVU is a Volvo B10M – the Shearings standard vehicle throughout the 1990s – fitted here with Van Hool Alizee body.

R903 YBA, another Volvo B10M, seen here in Truro on 27 April 2000, makes an interesting comparison with the previous photograph, being fitted with the later Van Hool Alizee T9 body.

Operating a tour based on Torquay, Plaxton Panther-bodied Volvo B10M W227 JBN, was spotted in Plymouth's Bretonside bus station on 10 August 2001. Bretonside was a bit of a Mecca for bus photographers, being filled with coaches of all shapes and sizes from all over the country, especially in the summer months, as well as the local service buses and express coaches.

Another north-western company to be seen frequently in my native West Country is Robinsons of Great Harwood. Photographed at Newquay Pearl on 9 August 2001, Plaxton Excalibur-bodied Volvo B10M S260 JFR wears the livery of the associated Holdsworth Holidays company.

Tyrer of Nelson was a small family-run business with a forty-year history. Seen in Skipton bus station on 3 April 2004, waiting its departure time for Preston, was their DAF SB220 YJ51 EKP, carrying an Ikarus Polaris body. Tyrer was taken over by Holmeswood of Rufford in 2013.

Whilst not being able to make any trips to Scotland during this period, I did still come across coaches from Scottish operators. Lanarkshire-based Bruce of Shotts were operating this National Express-liveried Bova Futura R101 PWR, on service 502 to Ilfracombe, when I photographed it leaving Taunton bus station on 17 August 2001.

The all-over black coaches of Park's of Hamilton are also a familiar sight nationwide. In 2000, Park's was the first operator to take delivery of Plaxton's new Paragon body, fitted to their standard Volvo B10M chassis. One of these vehicles was HSK 657, seen in Newquay on 11 August 2001 also carrying additional lettering for National Express.

A well-known operator that I only got to see a couple of times over the years was Pennine Motors of Gargrave. However, a visit to Skipton on 3 April 2004 provided me with an opportunity to photograph a number of the members of their fleet, including this former Go-Ahead Northern Dennis Dart, J613 KCU, fitted with Wright Handybus body – a style that I always thought looked a little dated.

Another of Pennine's Dennis Darts to be seen on that visit was P696 HND, carrying a Plaxton Pointer body. This vehicle was new to Meteor Parking at Heathrow Airport. It then served at Southampton Airport before finding its way to Pennine in 2004, via Ryder of Oldbury and Countryman of Ibstock.

Pennine also quite liked the Leyland National, as shown here by JIL 2428, formerly BYW 412V, again seen in Skipton on 3 April 2004. An interesting note here is that the distinctive roof pod has been removed.

Pride of the Dales operated into Skipton from its base at Grassington in Wharfedale. By the 2000s, low-floor Optare Solos, such as VIA 1647, seen here on 3 April 2004, had very much become the norm.

In 2001, National Holidays came under the ownership of Wallace Arnold, and vehicles were cascaded from the main Wallace Arnold fleet. Plaxton Premiere 350-bodied Volvo B10M M119 UWY moved to the National Holidays fleet in 1999, staying there until its withdrawal in 2005. It is seen in Newquay on 4 April 2002.

One of the great advantages for a bus enthusiast living in such a popular tourist area as the West Country is the opportunity to see and photograph coaches from all over the country on a frequent basis. Here, Abbotts of Leeming in North Yorkshire had sent their Irizar Century-bodied Scania R1 ABB for a holiday in Cornwall. It is seen on Cliff Road, Newquay on 9 August 2001.

K19 FTG, a Volvo B10M with Plaxton Excalibur body, was with its third owner by the time I photographed it in Bretonside bus station, Plymouth, on 22 August 2000. New to Flights Tours in 1993, it reached Gordons of Rotherham in 1998 via Johnson of Hodthorpe.

Moving away from Yorkshire area operators and into Lincolnshire we come to the well-known and well-respected company Delaine of Bourne. Always very smartly turned out, their Volvo B10B P112 RGS was attending the popular Wisley Rally, on 4 April 2004, when I photographed it. Carrying a Wright Renown body, it passed to Delaine from Sovereign Buses.

Low-floor double-deckers were much more in evidence with the smaller independent companies in the 2000s, and bus rallies were often a good place to photograph vehicles from operators one might not normally see. Again, attending the Wisley Rally, this time on 2 April 2006, was Delaine's AD04 OCT, a Volvo B7TL with an East Lancs Vyking body.

Moving across into Norfolk we come to the fleet of Chenery, based in Dickleburgh, south of Norwich. Chenery was a keen operator of the German-built Setra, employing them on the National Express workings. Here, R304 EEX, a Setra S250, is seen leaving Victoria coach station for Great Yarmouth on 5 January 2001.

Colchester could always be relied upon to produce an interesting selection of vehicles, as the following shots will show. Seen in the bus station on 12 August 2000 was G523 VYE, from the fleet of Carter of Ipswich. This Duple Dartliner-bodied Dennis Dart, formerly with London United as its DT23, was laying over before working to Hadleigh on service 755.

Cedric's of Wivenhoe operated a service from Brightlingsea to Colchester. In use on 12 August 2000 was ACM 705X, an ECW bodied Leyland Olympian that originated with Merseyside PTE as number 0031.

Chambers of Bures was founded in 1877, purchasing its first motor bus in 1918. Seen in Colchester High Street on 12 August 2000 was a slightly different beast, W91 HRT, a Scania N113DRB with an East Lancs Cityzen body, bound for Sudbury on service 758.

As well as bus services in the Sudbury area, Chambers also operate coach hires. Seen in Trafalgar Square on 23 February 2001 is S413VBJ, a Scania with a Van Hool Alizee T9 body.

Always a major presence in the Colchester area was Hedingham Omnibuses. Seen in the High Street on 12 August 2000 – a day that turned out to be quite productive photographically – is F150 LTW, Hedingham's only Leyland Lynx, making its way to Fordham.

Hedingham developed a liking for Bristol VRs, purchasing a large number as they became available. HJB 456W originated with my former local operator, Alder Valley. It is seen here in Colchester bus station, again on 12 August 2000, awaiting departure for Walton.

Caught on 12 August 2000 as it arrived in Colchester bus station on a 608 working to Halstead is Hedingham's M832 CVG, a Plaxton Pointer-bodied Volvo B6. Both Hedingham and Chambers joined the Go-Ahead Group in 2012.

1482 PP was new to Fishwick of Leyland as J9 JFS. Originally re-registered J158 OHG, this Van Hool Alizee-bodied DAF SB3000 found its way to the fleet of Galloway of Mendlesham by a circuitous route that took in four other operators before making its home in Suffolk. It is seen here entering Colchester bus station on 12 August 2000, whilst on a National Express working to London from Ipswich.

Burtons of Haverhill became part of the Tellings Golden Miller Group in 2003, operating in the TGM livery. In this shot, taken on 31 July 2004 at Reading station, we see W800 BCL, a Plaxton Panther-bodied Volvo B10M.

Definitely one of the more uncommon vehicles to be seen was this Ayats Atlantis, AJ03 LZA. Spotted at the Brighton Coach Rally in April 2004, it was owned by Cedar Coaches of Bedford.

Working for Universitybus of Hatfield at Watford Junction station on 31 May 2001, was Leyland Lynx G472PGE, seen here awaiting departure to the Hatfield campus of the University of Hertfordshire. Acquired from Whitelaw of Stonehouse in 1993, this vehicle stayed in the fleet until 2002. From 2005 the firm traded as Uno, adopting a brighter livery of pink and purple.

Also caught on 31 May 2001 at Watford Junction was P664 PNM, a Dennis Dart SLF with Wright Crusader body, working a service to Welwyn Garden City.

Richmond Coaches of Barley, near Royston in Hertfordshire, was established in 1946 and has remained in the Richmond family. Seen here within Heathrow Airport on 9 August 2000 is HDT 375, a three-axle Volvo B10M with Van Hool Alizee T9 body.

Station Hill was the main terminal point for bus services in Reading. Here, seen in September 2001 is B6R MT, a Mercedes-Benz 811D with Optare StarRider body from the fleet of Mott of Stoke Mandeville. Originally registered K935 GWR it was new to Ralphs of Langley, passing to Mott in 1996.

Chiltern Queens were a familiar sight around the Reading area for many years. Seen at Reading station on 29 May 2001, working a service to Wallingford, is F344 TSC, a Mercedes-Benz 811D with an Alexander body. Chiltern Queens service buses were usually red and cream, but TSC is wearing the green coach livery.

Proclaiming its 'Low Floor Easy Access' credentials at Reading station on 1 September 2001, before heading home to Woodcote, is Y313 KDP, one of three Volvo B6BLE with East Lancs Spryte bodies that Chiltern Queens bought in 2001. These vehicles were the last new buses bought by the firm as it unfortunately ceased trading in 2002.

Seen on Station Hill, Reading, on 16 February 2002, just a few short months before the demise of the company, is Chiltern Queens D504 NWG, a former Yorkshire Traction Mercedes-Benz L608D with an Alexander body.

Horseman of Reading has its origins in the well-known fleet of Smiths of Reading. Seen on Station Hill, Reading, on 2 October 2000 was L955 NWW, a Volvo B10M with Jonckheere Deauville 45 body bought from Wallace Arnold in 1998.

The Worldcom organisation operated a staff service from Reading station for about a year. Seen on 29 May 2001 was T441 EBD, a Dennis Dart SLF with Wright Crusader body.

Thames Travel was founded in 1998 and expanded fairly swiftly, partly through taking over services from firms such as Chiltern Queens. Seen on 29 May 2001 at Reading station, Y972 GPN, a Dennis Dart SLF with Plaxton Pointer 2 body, was just arriving from Wokingham on service 144. Thames Travel passed to the Go-Ahead Group in 2011.

Countywide Travel of Basingstoke took over a number of routes from Tillingbourne when that company folded, including a route from Aldershot to Reading, via Fleet. Seen at The Forbury, Reading, on 16 February 2002, is RL51 ZLO, a Mercedes-Benz Vario with a Plaxton Beaver 2 body. It subsequently operated under the *Fleet Buzz* name and was acquired by Stagecoach in 2011.

Tellings Golden Miller operated a number of bus services around South West London and Surrey, some of which were acquired from Capital Logistics. Seen here in the Central bus station at Heathrow Airport on 9 August 2000 is M80 TGM, a Plaxton Beaver-bodied Mercedes-Benz 709D on service 41 to Englefield Green.

Another Plaxton-bodied Mercedes-Benz in the TGM fleet was P702 LCF, this time a Vario O810 model. It is seen here on 31 July 2001 leaving Guildford's Friary bus station for Kingston on service 515, a route that more or less followed the route of the old Green Line service 715, which I used to use to travel on to and from my college in Kingston.

Seen in the Central bus station, on 9 August 2000, at Heathrow Airport on service 726 from Bromley South is TGM's W402 UGM, a Dennis Dart SLF with a dual-door Plaxton Pointer 2 body.

Working the same route on 24 May 2000 was W901 UJM, a Volvo B10BLE with an Alexander ALX300 body – one of seven bought for this service. It is seen here at Hampton Court, about to take the turn to its right towards Sunbury.

Tellings Golden Miller also operated a modern coach fleet, including W10 TGM, a German-built Setra S315GT, seen at Heathrow Airport on 9 August 2000.

Armchair Passenger Transport was initially a coach operator, becoming an operator of bus services as a contractor to London Regional Transport in 1990. Seen here in Kingston, on service 65 to Ealing Broadway, on 3 June 2000, is R420 SOY, a Volvo Olympian with Northern Counties Palatine 2 body. My college days in Kingston meant I used the 65 on occasions, worked then by Routemasters.

Seen on Hounslow High Street on 23 September 2000, bound for Isleworth on service 117, is Armchair's Plaxton-bodied Dennis Dart P27 MLE.

Another established coach operator who moved into bus operation was Limebourne Coaches. Seen here in Wimbledon on 1 June 2000, bound for Clapham Junction on service 156, is T415 LGP, a Dennis Dart SLF with Caetano Nimbus body. The following month Limebourne was purchased by Connex.

I never got the opportunity to photograph the vehicles of Blue Triangle actually in service in London. However, I did come across V909 FEC, a Dennis Trident with an East Lancs Lolyne body, at the Cobham Rally on 8 April 2001.

Thorpes of Wembley operated this Plaxton-bodied Dennis Dart SLF, KU52 YLB, on service 705 to Paddington. It is seen here rounding Hyde Park Corner on 1 September 2003. By now there was a ruling that the liveries of vehicles operating London Regional Transport services had to be 80 per cent red.

The London sightseeing market is a very intense one and produces some interesting vehicles. Seen here on Buckingham Palace Road on 5 January 2001 is AEC Routemaster LDS 236A, belonging to the Big Bus Company. This was originally RM272 in the London Transport fleet, registered VLT 272.

The Big Bus Company imported a number of three-axle double-deckers from the China Motor Bus Company of Hong Kong in the early 2000s, including Metrobus F153 UJN, photographed rounding Hyde Park Corner on 1 September 2003.

Hyde Park Corner is again the venue for another imported bus from Hong Kong, G991 FVX. Again converted to open-top, this is a Dennis Condor with a Duple Metsec body.

This time converted to partial open-top, G864 FVX is another Dennis Condor with Duple Metsec body. Seen again on 1 September 2003 at Hyde Park Corner, looking at the stormy clouds gathering, the passengers on the upper deck might have appreciated the cover!

The London tour market is a lucrative one, especially those catering for visitors from outside the UK. Seen at Hampton Court station on 14 June 2000, awaiting the return of its passengers visiting Hampton Court Palace on a CIE tour from Ireland, is W252 UGX, a Setra S315GT of Redwing.

Epsom Coaches moved into bus operation in 1986. Seen here laying over in West Croydon bus station on 1 June 2003 after working service 166 from Epsom is K321 GEW, a Marshall-bodied Dennis Dart, the only example of this combination they bought.

During 2003, Epsom Coaches rebranded their bus services as Quality Line. Seen in Kingston's Fairfield bus station, on 3 June 2003, and displaying this branding is S452 LGN, a Plaxton-bodied Mercedes-Benz Vario on service K9 to Epsom.

South of Croydon is Gatwick Airport, which has various bus services linking the terminals with long-stay car parks and hotels. An interesting vehicle employed on this work and seen on 1 August 2000 in Gatwick's dark and gloomy bus station, was V85 EAK, a Neoplan owned by Hallmark of Luton.

Another of Hallmark's vehicles engaged on airport/car park duties on 1 August 2000 was P204 RUM, a DAF SB220 with an Ikarus body, seen again in the shadows of the bus station.

Sunday operation of service 32 from Guildford to Redhill was interesting in 2000 and 2001 in that it was worked by Memory Lane Travel using preserved vehicles. Working the route on 26 March 2000, and seen in Guildford's Friary bus station, was LYF 377, a former Green Line RF type of 1951, complete with Green Line-style route boards for service 32 above the windows.

Seen at Dorking station on 2 September 2001, taking a turn on service 32, was 253 KTA, a 1962 Bristol MW6G with an ECW body, formerly Royal Blue 2270. These vehicles were very familiar to me from my childhood in Somerset in the 1960s and early '70s.

Coming full circle back to Guildford, it seems fitting that the last few photos in this book should be of two of my favourite companies, in this case the much-lamented Tillingbourne. TIL 1185 is a Volvo B10M with a Plaxton Derwent body, delivered new as K102 XPA. It is seen here in the Friary bus station on 26 October 2000 on service 32 from Redhill.

Also working on service 32 from Redhill on 26 October 2000 was R202 YOR, a Mercedes-Benz O405 with an Optare Prisma body. This vehicle was part of Tillingbourne's large investment in new vehicles in the 1990s.

A vehicle that I think was on hire to Tillingbourne when I saw it on 2 September 2000 was T421 ADN, an Optare MetroRider, seen here departing Guildford Friary bus station for Cranleigh on service 42.

Safeguard's second Dennis Dart, L265 EPD, like the first carrying a Plaxton Pointer body, is seen here on 31 July 2001 leaving Guildford Friary bus station for Park Barn.

A second-hand Dennis Dart in the Safeguard fleet, this time with Northern Counties Paladin body, was N611 WND, seen here on 26 October 2000 in Onslow Street, Guildford.

A final example of Safeguard's smart coach fleet is S503 UAK, a Dennis Javelin with a Plaxton Premiere 320 body, parked in Guildford Park Road on 25 February 2002.

Bibliography

Berry, Howard, *Roselyn of Cornwall: A Celebration of 70 Years Service: 1947 to 2017* (Chezbrook Publishing, 2017).

Burnett, George and Laurie James, *Tillingbourne: The Tillingbourne Bus Story* (Midhurst: Middleton Press, 1990).

James, Laurie, *Safeguard Coaches of Guildford* (Stroud: Amberley Publishing, 2014).